Interiors **Ugo di Pace**

di PACE

Interiors

UGO

RIZZOLI
NEW YORK

Interiors Ugo di Pace

First published in the
United States of America
in 2007 by
**Rizzoli International
Publications, Inc.**
300 Park Avenue South
New York, NY 10010
www.rizzoliusa.com

ISBN: 978-0-8478-3004-6
LCCN: 2007921703

Distributed to the U.S.
trade by Random House,
New York

Design
Alexandre Wollner
Design Production
Jorge Bastos
Alessandra Viude

Photography
Rômulo Fialdini
Lew Parrella (pages 74–76,
194–207)

Printed and bound in China

2007 2008 2009 2010 2011/10 9 8 7 6 5 4 3 2 1

Contents

The Poetry of the Architect

Ugo di Pace

Everything is Simultaneous in Modern Culture: Past, Present, and Future.
—Gio Ponti

The only protagonist of architecture is space: creating positive internal space from the negative element that is external space.
—Bruno Zevi

These concepts have greatly influenced my professional life. An architect sculpts space, in his way, and the forms are infinite. Thus, talent and imagination spread their wings and soar to immense heights; intrinsic to this flight is a capacity to dream, and the dream becomes poetry—this is the poetry of the architect.

This is how I can best express my thoughts with regard to what this book is. It covers my design production of the last five years, and includes some older work that embodies my line of conduct, which is timeless and follows no fashions. I am, by the way, *against* fashion!

My interiors are the consequence of my architecture, and their decoration is "non-decoration" since, whenever possible, I try to avoid giving the air of a "decorated house" to my compositions.

The protagonists of my interiors are works of art, ancient or modern, including sculptures, paintings, and architectural elements, whereas the actual furniture, such as upholstered articles, tables, et cetera, exists only for functional reasons.

I like the contrast between pieces from different periods and cultures, and composing them in such a way as to give the impression that they have been there forever.

Scenography is another aspect of my work. I think that life is a wonderful theater in which we are the actors, so when I think about composing a house, I think about the scenography of the play unfolding in each one, in which the home's owners are the leading characters, living in their own story. Each one of us plays countless roles in life, which is why we are the actors in this extraordinary show.

I like designing some of the furniture as well, combining ancient fragments with modern elements; the spirit of the piece is as important for me as its appearance.

The lighting in my work is fundamental: I see a difference between merely lighting something and having an effect that enables me to create a magical environment that by night entirely transforms the atmosphere.

Some people have played an important role in my life as an artist and professional. I owe my humanistic education to one of the greatest Italian thinkers of the twentieth century, the philosopher Benedetto Croce, who—through his dissertations on esthetics, history, and poetry—led me to think about the reasons for my own existence. I also owe my education in art history to Roberto Longhi, a fine art critic and historian. I owe what I know about the many technical aspects of painting to a great Venetian painter active in Brazil, Vittorio Gobbis. I owe everything I know about how one should face the world of the arts and its various branches to my friend Pietro Maria Bardi. I am also indebted to my wife Vera, who is endowed with an extraordinary critical sense and has always brought my attention to important details, improving my ideas and reining me back into the reality of things.

I learned a great deal during the time I lived in Rome, from 1963 to 1968, directing Studio A, an art gallery in a fifteenth-century building on Via del Babuino, in partnership with Pietro Maria Bardi, José Gudiol, and Mimi Sironi (widow of the painter Mario Sironi). During our time at Studio A, several important exhibitions of works by Renoir, Bonnard, Vuillard, Modigliani, Picasso, and many others were held, some in collaboration with George Wildenstein, one of the twentieth century's finest art dealers.

In São Paulo, I also headed the Arte Hispânica Gallery, in partnership with Bardi, whose collection had unique pieces from nearly all ancient and modern cultures.

My experience with galleries and antiques dealerships helped a great deal as I began to look for works of art for my projects and clients.

With regard to style, I believe that each artist has to exercise his own. Interpreting a style from past ages in the world we now live in, in the third millennium, will always become more and more relative. Of course, everyone has his own personal choices, but a replica will always raise doubts concerning the issues of balance and harmony of taste. For me, a love of the past is important—provided it contributes to creating the future.

—Ugo di Pace

The Calligrapher of Space

Nirlando Beirão

Art is intuition, and intuition is individuality . . . . Art is governed entirely by imagination; its only riches are images. Art does not classify objects, nor pronounce them real or imaginary, nor qualify them, nor define them. Art feels and represents them. Nothing more.
—Benedetto Croce, *Esthetic as Science of Expression and General Linguistic*

Ugo di Pace approaches each of his remarkable projects with a unique modesty. He has designed a theater in São Paulo, a four-story apartment building in Paris, a penthouse in New York, and many other buildings, but has never been one of those interior designers who proudly insist upon blatant recognition. He simply replaces the label of "talent" with that of "personality." Di Pace is, curiously, most reluctant to find himself in the limelight, even in regard to this volume, which was in principle meant to be only about him.

He prefers instead to credit two of his closest masters. This deference is best understood in light of the proverbial nobility, nurtured by an education of Proustian refinement, into which di Pace was born. He grew up in a highly artistic environment—influenced by his father's architectural practice and his erudite mother's work in music and literature—in Naples, a city of Baroque stateliness and princely palazzi. Summer escapades in Capodimonte filled his adolescent senses with the aroma of lush climbing plants, framing infinite possibilities visible through large ancestral windows looking out over the vastness of history.

First and foremost is his earliest mentor, professor Pietro Maria Bardi, whom he met upon his definitive move to Brazil in 1951. Their friendship was cultivated in shared conversations, dreams, and projects—including the Studio A gallery in Rome—throughout the sixties, at the height of the dolce vita years. On one occasion the two of them, architect and critic, were on a pilgrimage to the National Gallery in London when *il Professore* stopped in front of a small Renaissance painting with a golden background by a Flemish painter, if I recall correctly, not half as boisterous as the nearby Turners, Rembrandts, and Botticellis. Bardi stopped in his tracks, took his friend by the arm, and simply said, "Now, see, *this* is an elegant picture."

An elegant painting. Elegant art. The critical canon usually celebrates masterpieces, exuberant canvases, garish panels, monumental sculptures, revolutionary experiments, or extravagant installations, but the prolific creator of the São Paulo Art Museum preferred elegance. Perhaps this is a simple idea, but it is nevertheless capable of lighting a fuse, illuminating a definitive message about art, life, and the world for sensitive souls like di Pace. Indeed, elegance is a notion that should never be overlooked, especially if one has to deal, as an architect is expected to, with concepts such as beauty, truth, pleasure, utility, agreeableness, and moral appropriateness.

Di Pace also pays tribute to a master he has revered for many years, as a declared disciple, while working on many projects to create a well-designed coexistence of space, light, atmosphere, topography, objects, and, of course, people. At this point, you will no doubt be thinking, "So what? There's nothing new here." This is the typical response, made with banal ease, to any and all architecture. The difference, however, is that di Pace's architecture is underpinned by his readings of Benedetto Croce and his lengthy exposure to the thoughts and work of this fellow southern Italian, a self-taught historian, literary critic, journalist, politician, and philosopher who showed the young di Pace, who was already a lover of form and color, the path to a complete consciousness of beauty.

Art, according to Croce, is the primary degree of cognitive function. It is individual awareness, intuition, and imagination, but ends up generating a collective code of knowledge. Art provides a cornerstone for knowledge, and this leads us to a field near and dear to di Pace: there is no architecture without art, without a vision of beauty. In Croce's system, which is both anti-academic and anti-metaphysical, these categories are interwoven on the palette of experience. Art precedes architecture. Esthetics does not exist without ethics. Reason and feeling are not contradictory, but rather complementary. Yet the philosophical exercise of experience does not exclude the power of abstraction. It is precisely because of this that we are endowed with spirit—to abstractly extend the frontiers of experience.

It is natural for a visionary designer, guided in his architectural practice by the same integrity of concept and vision with which Croce harmonized his philosophical doctrine, to blush when confronted with the panorama surrounding him—a field termed, variously, interior architecture, interior design, or decoration. Architecture based on art and illuminated by knowledge is one thing; what di Pace calls "furnituring," referring to decoration used as filler, as commercial garbage, or as a contortionist exercise to assuage a bad conscience (be it the client's or the designer's), is another thing altogether.

According to di Pace, "When you have a structured interior architecture project, strictly speaking, you wouldn't even need furniture." Furniture is a consequence, a function and result of the design and its space, hence often tragic attempts at certain impossible dialogues become clear—for instance, a regular cupboard juxtaposed with an execrable sculpture. "It's as if the whole setting starts to shake," he concludes, with the know-how of someone born at the foot of Vesuvius. Moreover, it is always advisable to be suspicious of a profusion of ruffles, surface linings, transatlantic sofas, pseudo-Moroccan pouffes, and devices originating in the arbitrary sphere of mere fetish.

Croce's philosophy upholds the ideal of an art that is "controlled passion" transformed into "serene contemplation"; if there is any one unshakeable conviction in di Pace's at times skeptical heart, it is the belief in the hegemony, within any proposed setting, of the work of art. According to the architect, "It's a spontaneous, inexplicable, magical fact that moves through the language of the unconscious . . . . The work of art appears and imposes itself. It communicates per se. It enunciates beauty. It changes the environment, which then ceases to be anonymous." Thus, the "serene contemplation" referred to by Croce is established, advancing in a direction quite opposite that of nouveau-riche exhibitionism and self-important propagandizing.

While di Pace is convinced, much like Charles Baudelaire, that where works of art are concerned taste can be discussed, quality cannot. It is not that he wishes to force a Picasso or a duly authenticated Doric capital from 200 BC upon anyone; a chair, a discreet sculpture, or a painting by a promising artist can imbue the architectural space with the same imperious harmony of an ancient Flemish tapestry, a Portinari, an architectural fragment, a Roman column, or a perspective of arches. As gallery owner, antiques dealer, and collector, di Pace finds his strongest inspiration in the ancient Greek and Roman worlds. Throughout his formative years, he drank from the fountains of Bernini and the images of De Sica. "But," he reiterates, "for me, art is art, and my references are universal."

If the drawing board (or the computer) of any interior architect invariably shows the materialization of a dialogue between client and creator, desire and imagination, di Pace belongs to the sort that does not hesitate to point out, right from the start, the limits of his malleability. "I will not do anything I do not believe in," he says, following the first commandment of those who approach architecture with a distinct morality. "Whatever I do has my style. It's a personality issue. I do not fight my own history. I do not believe in the legend that claims an architect translates into design whatever someone asks for. Nobody translates anything. I do what I know how to do. What I don't know, others will be capable of doing."

In line with the values he espouses in both his work and life, di Pace still believes in traits such as honor and authenticity. "I love my profession enough to have respect for myself and not renounce my choices, even when I have to pay a very high price for them," he says. He scorns banality, hypocrisy, fads, easy applause, and an evident vulgarization of the concept of talent, which is increasingly ascribed to those who lack it. Ugo di Pace is no longer an adolescent, but no one can say he fears being burnt by the flame of sensibility and gallantly continues venturing into the vortex of imagination. "My project is myself," he repeats. Like handwriting, it is useless to try to disguise it, as each person has his own.

Interiors **Ugo di Pace**

The material gathered in these special gray pages belongs to works created more than twenty years ago, whereas the ones that follow cover later works, from the last five years. They illustrate the common thread running through the project language and show that the character of the composition is timeless, the older projects remaining valid to this day.

Residential Interior
São Paulo, 1975

Instead of doors, the public areas of the home are divided by partitioning walls that can be rearranged according to the occasion.

An eighteenth-century Brussels tapestry; a pair of eighteenth-century blackamoor figures.

The entrance corridor; a Tang dynasty Chinese sculpture.

Tondo by Marc Nattier; eighteenth-century Tuscan table; seventeenth-century Venetian painting by Longhi; eighteenth- and nineteenth-century Chinese objects.

Gallery Nightclub
São Paulo, 1978

Restaurant detail with eighteenth-century columns salvaged from a demolished building.

Detail of a seventeenth-century cast-iron réchaud.

View of the nightclub, including the orchestra, stage, and large display window with a trompe l'oeil panel.

The entrance staircase to the restaurant, with an eighteenth-century Italian sculpture.

Residential Interior
São Paulo, 1974

Interior design with pieces of art from the owner's collection.

Corner with an eighteenth-century table; an eighteenth-century Italian sculpture.

View into an adjoining room; a set of marble obelisks and Italian marble sculpture in front of an eighteenth-century mirror.

Large eighteenth-century panel; Louis XV chairs; Louis XVI stool; pair of nineteenth-century columns with girandoles.

Architectural and Interior Design in Honor of Giorgio de Chirico
São Paulo, 1970

This project was inspired by Giorgio de Chirico's metaphysical compositions.

Arcangelo Ianelli painting; table with seventeenth-century columns, Gio Pomodoro sculpture; faux-marble polychrome wooden portals with mirror.

Tondo by Tito de Alencastro reflected in rear door; seventeenth-century Peruvian table.

A seventeenth-century Chinese tapestry between two portals.

Residential Architecture and Interior Design
São Paulo, 1968

This is one of Ugo di Pace's homes.

Large eighteenth-century Brussels tapestry; eighteenth-century Italian Baroque console.

View of a bedroom with an eighteenth-century
Empire bed.

A two-sided fireplace through which a sixteenth-century Ravenstein painting is seen; an eighteenth-century Portuguese sculpture.

Garden with a fountain built into the wall;
a nineteenth-century pre-Raphaelite sculpture.

Residential Interior
São Paulo, 1974

This same house also appears, with later renovations completed in 2005, on pages 174–81.

Ugo di Pace Interior Design Office and Showroom
São Paulo, 1980

The mezzanine and visible air-conditioning system; this system and the rest of the office structure are supported by iron railings.

View of the lower room.

Mezzanine with a nineteenth-century railway station balustrade.

Residential Interior
Milan, 1972

The rooms are continuous, linked by a sequence of arches.

Detail of the living room.

The living room and office; the library lined with sheets of steel and leather.

Another corner of the living room, with sofas atop a masonry base, steel skirting boards, and low tables.

Antiques Store Interior
São Paulo, 1989

The iron facade, painted black.

Interior view, showing the entire steel railing structure and mobile canvas panels, which create a background for the works of art.

Residential Architecture and Interior Design
São Paulo, 1973

The rooms are continuous and are not constrained by interior separating walls.

The living room and fireplace, with an ideal division created by Baroque eighteenth-century columns in the background.

Concrete staircase leading to the upper floor; white cement flooring with a design that echoes wooden floorboards; iron and glass doors.

Residential Architecture and Interior Design
São Paulo, 1974

Materials salvaged during the demolition of an eighteenth-century factory were used for this new construction, including wooden beams, old stones, and bricks.

The interior as seen from the garden.

The living room, with a painting by Pablo Picasso and a tondo by Andrea del Sarto.

View of the fireplace; dining table supported by an eighteenth-century capital.

Residential Architecture and Interior Design for an Archaeology Collector
São Paulo, 1968

Painting and furniture from the Italian Renaissance.

Large room with double-height ceilings and mezzanines visible to the left and right; the floor is a special cement mixed with marble powder and aluminum oxide.

The library, lined in red suede with black iron columns.

View of the fireplace room from the mezzanine.

Residential Architecture and Interior Design

São Paulo, 1971

The game room and library, entirely lined with steel plates and graphite suede; the coffee table and game table are also steel.

Entrance hall with a view of the garden through the back window.

View of an interior with wide masonry sofas and a seventeenth-century Tuscan portal.

One of the patios.

View of the swimming pool, large picture windows, and staircase in concrete and glass, leading up to the mezzanine.

Residential Interior
São Paulo, 1970

This project was the first home of my son, Luiz Carlos.

The entrance corridor with a large pen-and-ink drawing by Darcy Penteado; door and column in faux marble; marble floor with a pink and white diamond-shaped pattern.

The living room with a fireplace, a mirrored wall, and pink silk sofas and curtains.

Residential Interior
Istanbul, 1989

Entrance door.

Dining room table designed by Ugo di Pace featuring seventeenth-century capitals and a wooden Baltic pine beam; eighteenth-century Brussels tapestry.

The living room.

Room with double-height ceilings and mezzanine.

Residential Penthouse Interior
New York, 1988

Staircase leading to the bedrooms; sixteenth-century Italian portal.

The living room, with panoramic views to the east and west.

Residential Architecture and Interior Design for an Art Collector
São Paulo, 1973

Two partial views of the living room.

The grand entrance gallery; salvaged eighteenth-century stone portals.

Part of the mezzanine.

The veranda and a staircase lined with Portuguese tiles.

View of the living room and mezzanine.

The swimming pool.

Interiors **Ugo di Pace**

Offices of Di Pace & di Pace Associados
São Paulo, 2001

This office is a steel structure with lateral supports and an unimpeded view of the open span at the building's center. This allows for total freedom in rearranging the interior layout, and also permits future interventions without major remodeling.

Tuscan furniture from the seventeenth-century; a painting by Francesco Guardi.

Nineteenth-century Biedermeier divan; table in background made from nineteenth-century neo-Gothic fragments.

On the back wall, a pair of paintings by Carlo Maratta; in the center, a grisaille by Martins Geezaertz.

View of an eighteenth-century Manueline table in the back corner.

Two views of the mezzanine and lower level; paintings by Eugene Boudin, Il Mirandolese, and Van Balen.

Views of the lower level with an abstract painting by Valadares on the left; pair of fifteenth-century Italian columns; painting by John Guerin; sixteenth-century Florentine table; seventeenth-century Roman sculpture; sixteenth-century framed mirror.

Another view of the mezzanine and lower level. Above, eighteenth-century Neapolitan sculpture; abstract painting by Aguillar. Below, painting by Alan Davie; large eighteenth-century Sicilian potiche from a unique series of six.

Paintings by Pan Cherry and Vittorio Gobbis;
note the iron structure and balustrade.

Ground floor view.

Duplex Penthouse Apartment Interior

São Paulo, 2004

Pair of nineteenth-century Ionian columns; seventeenth-century Florentine potiche, with a collection of ivory walking sticks; Roman sculpture from the second century BC in front of a Genovese mirror.

This design features a broad, bright, fluid space, with a minimum number of walls built around a central area with a double-height ceiling around which all the other rooms are arranged.

The living room and entrance corridor.

The central portion of the public space, with a twenty-foot ceiling height, to house a collection of objects from various times and cultures, ranging from ancient Rome to colonial Brazil: to the left, a painting by Pablo Picasso; in the middle, chairs by Alvar Aalto and Redmille.

A 1935 chair by Ludwig Mies van der Rohe at center; to the right, a sculpture by Redmille.

A home theater and library, built with eighteenth-century Spanish stone columns; on the right, a sculpture by Luca della Robbia; a 1940 Broier table; eighteenth-century Swedish chairs.

A sculpture by Prosper d'Epinay on the left; on the right, eighteenth-century Brazilian folk art; armchair by Vico Magistretti.

A low bar made with one hundred Delft tiles manufactured in 1600; on the left, a seventeenth-century large Baroque Venetian chair and signed Louis XVI armchairs; painting by Domingos Toledo Pisa.

Partial view of the living room from the mezzanine; on the wall between the two round windows is a seventeenth-century Baroque German sculpture.

On the left, a view of the dining room with a seventeenth-century Tuscan portal in the background. In the center, a room with a double-height ceiling and staircase leading to the upper floor; note the freedom created by the lack of doors and windows.

Chapel for a Collector of Sacred Art

São Paulo, 2003

This project was designed around the existing structure of one of São Paulo's most important residences; we chose to create a light structure with a large open span, an area fully integrated into the house's traditional exterior, but with a contemporary interior.

The design highlights the quadrangular shape of the segmented arched ceiling and provides a full view of the arrangement of the collection, which ranges from the seventeenth to nineteenth centuries. In the center, a pair of eighteenth-century Peruvian stools; pink and white Italian marble floors.

A large seventeenth-century Spanish portal from Seville, resituated here with no reconstruction and supported by two lateral iron railings, framing a fifteenth-century sculpture by Benedetto de Maiano; at the back, a seventeenth-century Colombian carving.

An Italian seventeenth-century altar crowned by a sixteenth-century image of Christ from Minas Gerais.

Four eighteenth-century carvings by Frei Valentim.

Residence for a Prominent Art Collector

São Paulo, 2005

This interior design has a highly scenographic character, lending transparency to the surroundings and allowing the greenery of the gardens to enter the atmosphere from all sides. It was specially designed to hold an extraordinary art collection ranging from the French Empire to the twentieth century.

The stagelike entrance corridor: to the left, a sixteenth-century verdure tapestry; at the back, in the garden, a composition of plants forming a backdrop of natural greenery.

View of the dining room with a seventeenth-century tapestry framed by a pair of oversize eighteenth-century candleholders.

Partial view of the living room with a nineteenth-century Biedermeier divan between a pair of eighteenth-century iron vases.

An eighteenth-century Central European armoire; to the left, a sculpture by Bruno Giorgi; in the background, the entrance gallery and garden.

View of the living room and garden with paintings by Picasso, Rubens, Toulouse-Lautrec, Portinari, and Renoir; coffee table designed by Ugo di Pace featuring sixteenth-century Tuscan stone fragments, iron, and glass.

Seaside Residence
São Paulo, 2001

In this beach house, built by G. Mariutti, our interventions aimed to create viewpoints that enhance particular angles of the house. We tried to make the interiors lighter, lending them a more modern and luminous character.

The chief concern in the main living room was to provide it with more light and greater transparency, so as to make its atmosphere as bright as possible. The mirror on the wall above the fireplace is designed to those same ends.

View of the living room, a minimalist composition with a few strong pieces, such as the pair of marble capitals; at the back, a central stone table and Roman sculpture. On the left are nineteenth-century Capo di Monte vases.

In this room, we created corners for reading, writing, watching television, and listening to music. Between the columns, a set of shelves for books and objects was designed. The contemporary paintings, in pale shades, make the walls seem lighter.

In the side room, a view of a lateral gallery.

Reading corner with a view of the garden patio.

View of the bar looking toward the swimming pool.

View through the bar, opening out to the gallery framed by climbing plants.

Residence for an Art Aficionado
São Paulo, 2002

In this home, we worked with a large open span, openings to the exterior, and a range of ceiling heights made possible by the mixed concrete and steel structure. The spaces are airy, and glass, the main architectural element, integrates the interior, garden, and landscape.

Seventeenth-century table next to a pair of sixteenth-century stone columns; on the table, nineteenth-century plaster sculptures and a tenth-century Romanesque marble sculpture; painting by Alan Hekel.

The entrance corridor, with ancient Roman fragments embedded in the wall; large eighteenth-century faience amphora (from a series of six).

ALGARDI

View of the mezzanine and lower level: below, on the extreme left, a corner of the lap pool. The ceiling here is twenty feet high.

The lower living room.

View from the lower level through to the dining room and mezzanine; the upper living room is on the right.

Next to the sofa, a pair of seventeenth-century capitals; a glimpse of the lap pool.

An eighteenth-century Italian table; a grotesque armchair.

Another view of the lower level and mezzanine.

Partial view of the lap pool; upholstered furniture; a pair of eighteenth-century Baroque Italian sculptures.

A forty-foot-long heated lap pool; the sculptures on the iron supports are a single work completed in Italy in 2003 by Beto Lovatelli.

Bookshelves between eighteenth-century Neapolitan columns and an eighteenth-century painting by G. P. Pannini.

In the dining room, a mirror-covered back wall supports a large marble capital that holds the console table's glass top; table designed by Ugo di Pace featuring a pair of marble capitals and glass; chairs lined with green velvet.

A 1920 armchair lined with zebra skin and cashmere; in the background, a nineteenth-century African sculpture.

Another view of the upper room.

View of the upper room with the dining room toward the back; bookshelves with first- and second-century BC Roman sculptures. Detail of the scagliola table with marble fragments.

Detail of the upper room and large picture window framing a fountain with eighteenth-century marble elements.

The upper living room viewed from the dining room mezzanine.

Views of the rear facade and swimming pool.

The garden pavilion.

Triplex Apartment for Three-time Formula 1 Grand Prix Champion

São Paulo, 2006

This penthouse has an open span between internal columns, and is laterally supported to provide total freedom for a changing interior layout, so as to integrate the three floors in one continuous space.

The composition of this three-floor apartment was achieved exclusively with pieces from Ugo di Pace's collection.

Detail of the staircase leading to the third floor.

Architectural detail showing a partial view of the upper and lower rooms.

Views of the lower room and the rhythmic arches of the upper room.

A seventeenth-century table crowned by an eighteenth-century marble statue; sixteenth-century Tuscan furniture.

View of the lower room; in the center, a pair of nineteenth-century Italian amphorae.

Two views of the lower living room.

A third-floor room, with a panorama of São Paulo.

Detail of the staircase leading to the first floor.

Architectural details.

The third-floor pool and solarium, with retracting roof.

Apartment for a Prominent Brazilian Legal Expert

São Paulo, 2003

In designing this apartment, the rooms were integrated as much as possible in order to highlight its focal points without altering the preexisting structure.

View of the living and dining rooms to the right; to the left, the luncheon room.

The living room, with a pair of eighteenth-century Ionic wooden columns.

The entrance gallery.

On the left, a painting by Fukushima and an eighteenth-century Venetian grotesque flowerbox; on the right, a painting by Tarsila do Amaral and a seventeenth-century Italian wooden sculpture of Bacchus.

At the back, seventeenth-century wainscoting; a low bar lined with the same wainscoting and a painting by Di Cavalcanti.

In the foreground, a seventeenth-century marble capital between a pair of Vico Magistretti armchairs; in the background, a seventeenth-century Tuscan table crowned by a first-century BC Roman torso; in the center, a sculpture by Alberto Frioli.

Residence for a Young Business Couple
São Paulo, 2002

In this preexisting house, our intervention included brightening the rooms and integrating them as much as possible. Without altering the home's main structure, we opened the interior space to the exterior, increasing its internal brightness and integrating the garden and home.

The living room.

View of the entrance corridor lined by eighteenth-century Italian columns.

Glass shelves housing a collection of nineteenth-century antique toys.

View of the entrance corridor and the brushed steel door.

The library; fitted into the mirrored wall is a two-sided fireplace with a view toward the garden.

Wooden library with eighteenth-century stone columns and a Louis XVI Swedish desk.

View of the living room, with the entrance corridor and office in the background.

A low bar made with seventeenth-century marble tiles, and a painting by Gustavo Rosa.

Residence for a São Paulo Banker
São Paulo, 2001

This project involved a radical renovation, increasing the floor area by one-third. With a structure that combined steel, concrete, zinc, and a lot of glass, we transformed a house that was previously devoid of style into a contemporary home with expansive integrated spaces, ceilings of various heights, and large openings to unite interior and exterior.

The large living room, with a staircase leading to the upper level and the dining room on the right.

The library with its column supports; a pair of nineteenth-century polychromed lamps; a marble, steel, and glass coffee table, bearing a nineteenth-century African sculpture.

View of the dining room with an eighteenth-century Coromandel screen in the background; dining room table designed by Ugo di Pace featuring nineteenth-century Art Nouveau terra-cotta elements.

The dining room.

To the right, through the dining room, another view of the library.

A low bar made with eighteenth-century terra-cotta tiles and a painting by Mário Gruber.

View of the living room with a double-height ceiling, movie screen, and floor-to-ceiling bookshelf.

Above, view of the bedroom behind the movie screen.

View of the staircase leading to the upper level.

The living room by night, with a double-height ceiling and bookshelves holding a collection of sixteenth- and seventeenth-century fragments.

The pool patio.

The entrance corridor.

Duplex Apartment for an Advertising Executive

São Paulo, 2004

This apartment is in one of our flexible-plan buildings and is an example of our solution for dealing with interior space, with large, integrated areas full of natural light.

View of the living room: table designed by Ugo di Pace featuring sixteenth-century wood, marble, and glass; Louis XIII chair with period tapestry.

View of the dining room; table with a seventeenth-century terra-cotta fragment and glass, designed by Ugo di Pace.

Another view of the living room; bookcase with antique objects, and pair of eighteenth-century Piranesi etchings.

Interior view with staircase leading down to the lower level and an eighteenth-century Italian marble sculpture.

View of the staircase; column held by a support from the lower level; marble sculpture; paintings by Burri and Giorgio de Chirico.

The living room, with a low bar on the left.

Residence for a Restaurant Entrepreneur
São Paulo, 2001

The living room, with double-height ceiling; on the wall, a pair of seventeenth-century Brussels tapestries from a series depicting Samson's tasks.

In this project we used a combined steel and concrete structure to work with the interior and exterior spaces as if they were sculpture. We created areas with a freeform floor plan, different ceiling heights, and large openings to capture a lot of natural light, which changes the feel of each space according to the time of day.

Eighteenth-century quartzite basin framed by a large picture window with a view of the garden.

The living room, facing the lower portion of the fireplace, with a view of the mezzanine, showing a long sofa; white cement and marble powder floor with a design that echoes wooden floors.

Staircase with iron railings leading to the mezzanine, with a view of all three levels.

View of the dining room; table with an eighteenth-century iron-capital base and glass top.

The iron cupola, glass top, and granite floor are balanced to create a geometric game; the fountain's water becomes a continuation of the floor.

The dining room, with seventeenth-century chairs.

Views of the rear facade and the pavilion, with the swimming pool between them.

Partial view of the living room as seen from the garden.

La Tambouille Restaurant
São Paulo, 2002

In our commercial projects, and the restaurants in particular, we always try to compose well-integrated settings that nevertheless offer distinct perspectives, creating a romantic aura aimed at invoking a pleasant sense of surprise and conveying different atmospheres inspired by my ancestral roots in Naples and Capri.

Wall with a fountain and ancient marble fragments, properly showing the eighteenth-century stone basin, all framed by an arch of blue-and-white tiles.

Central room, showing the floor lined with tiles reproduced from an original nineteenth-century Neapolitan design. In the background, the chafing dish.

View of the interior rooms.

A mirrored corner with an eighteenth-century Venetian console and clock cachepot from Compagnie des Indes. Two portraits, of a man and woman, indicate the respective toilets.

The central room as seen through the veranda.

Another interior view.

View of the larger room, with a sixteenth-century Spanish portal and terra-cotta cachepots on each side.

View of the fountain, chafing dish, and veranda.

Looking through a set of arches to the veranda, and a large cachepot (one from a series of six).

Residence for a Prominent Publisher

São Paulo, 2006

For this project in the traditional Jardins district of São Paulo, our preservation of the house's preexisting style fortuitously allowed a complete renovation of the rooms to create new internal spaces. We redesigned the old part of the home almost entirely, using steel structures to integrate the environments and create large open plans and openings to the exterior, thereby integrating the garden and house, and bringing more natural light to the interior.

Views of the entrance hall with a seventeenth-century marble fountain and the staircase leading to the apartment above. The ceiling is twenty-one feet high.

The passage from the living room to the great hall through a pair of nineteenth-century wooden Ionian columns; on the left, a painting by Tulio Costa.

The living room and hall.

The living room and central gallery.

View of upholstered furniture; seventeenth-century stone side table next to sofa; table beneath a mirror; a Ming-dynasty Chinese figure; on the right, a low bar with eighteenth-century terra-cotta carvings.

The dining room, with a painting by
Roberto Donatelli.

The luncheon room.

Dining room table designed by Ugo di Pace with a large copper base, marble, steel tubes, and glass. On the wall, an eighteenth-century verdure tapestry.

View of the living room, with an eighteenth-century Florentine scagliola coffee table.

Library bookshelves with nineteenth-century wooden columns and a game table.

Detail of the library.

Living room detail, with a painting by Valadares.

Left and right facades of the house, with the fitness room in front and the entertainment room above.

Residence for a Financier
São Paulo, 2006

This interior design aimed to free up as much space as possible, making the most of the surroundings' transparency and integrating the gardens to the left and the right. Some of the artworks were key to creating atmosphere.

Several passages between the living room and the entrance hall, whose ambience is set by the large Cumiera sculpture in English copper.

Two views of the large living room, with an eighteenth-century English trumeau between two large paintings by K. Schmidt and two chairs; pair of Chinese nineteenth-century coffee tables.

Detail of a mirror and an eighteenth-century English table.

A pair of chinoiserie chairs and nineteenth-century Italian sculpture.

Detail of the living room view toward the garden.

Detail of Chinese coffee tables with zebra-skin carpets.

Another view of the living room.

A Chinese table from the Chi'en-Lung period.

A large eighteenth-century Brussels verdure tapestry.

Composition with Chinese coffee tables: Compagnie des Indes tureen; English silver objects, including George III candlesticks. To the right, a Louis XV bombé commode and a painting by Vicente do Rego Monteiro.

Residence for a Prominent Jewelry Designer

São Paulo, 2006

In designing the interiors of this São Paulo home, our main concern was the essential character of the pieces and maintaining the greatest possible visual clarity, in order to highlight pieces such as the Vico Magistretti armchairs, the Cassina sofas, and the centerpieces of the collection—sculptures by Kreisberg and Rodin.

The living room, with windows opening onto the garden.

Another view of the living room, with Vico Magistretti chairs and the dining room in the background.

View of a stark white sculpture by Franz Krajcberg and a bust by Rodin.

The living room, with a deep black sculpture
by Franz Krajcberg.

Living room view toward the entrance hall and entertainment room, with a painting by Flavio Sholles in the background.

House
São Paulo, 2007

In deciding to design this house—with its spectacular panorama overlooking an urban landscape, on terrain crossed by a river, lush with exuberant vegetation—I thought about expressing in its design the sum of my dreams and the results of my experiences.

If asked to define residential architecture with an axiom, I would say it is created not only to shelter its inhabitants from the external environment, but also (and above all) to make them content within that environment. In addition to other considerations, architecture exists to be looked at. Hence, within this house, the aim was to create a fantasy home in which volumes are transformed into exciting architectural acts.

Two elements were the primary references for the aesthetics and scenography of this project: a large external wall filled with plants such that it resembles a forest; and a vast staircase that reminds me of a house I have always admired, the Casa Malaparte on the island of Capri.

The transparency of the structure enables one to view the verdant outdoor wall from all sides; the facade is made entirely of glass, and the interior has virtually no walls or doors. The view of the large staircase is also extremely important, as it is a key point of the volumetric aspect of the house's design.

Panoramic view of the upper patio.

The house as seen from the garden.

View of part of the garden.

Another garden view.

The home has an area of 28,000 square feet distributed over a generous, two-story social area with a double-height ceiling about twenty-four feet high, plus a mezzanine from which the room below is visible. The service areas are also fairly large, and include a kitchen, a dining room for the staff, a laundry, and three en-suite staff bedrooms. There are another three apartments adjacent to the garage, which can house twenty cars, in addition to a wine cellar, pantry, and other necessities. The third floor is reserved for five large en-suite bedrooms complete with walk-in closets and full baths, all of which open onto a grand patio as if this were a Pompeian house. Each room and the patio have an open view of the surrounding scenery.

All volumes are composed according to Euclidian geometry and are devoid of any forced decoration, thereby embodying the maxim that essentiality is a virtue—and therefore not an ephemeral aspect of the work.

The interior decoration was also carried out according to a personal vision, and interprets current global behaviors, which are so rapidly changing as to perplex our judgment of what should or should not be done. The composition obeys a chronological criterion, combining works of art from the fifteenth century to the present, arranged in a spontaneous manner, freely composed, with no predefined layout. Many pieces assume a function quite different from their original conception—a large Madeira vine root, for instance, becomes a comfortable chair—and such surprises emphasize the home's fantastical qualities.

Finally, this project was a collaboration with Gilberto Elkis on the landscape architecture, Antonio Carlos Mingroni in the lighting design, and Eliane Sicis in the use of the extraordinary finishing materials.

The house as seen from the garden at night.

A night view of the front facade, showing the large staircase and part of the ecological wall.

A corner of the house at night.

The right-hand side of the house, showing the upper and the lower pool.

Entrance hall showing, on the right, a twenty-meter-long, emerald-colored lap pool, lined with Sicis mosaic; in front, a pivoting mirrored door enables one to create several trompe l'oeil effects.

The lower part of the living room: on the left, the ecological wall, and on the right, part of the garden.

Night view of the ecological wall and of the pool lined with Sicis mosaic—the architecture of the wall recalls ruderal plants on the land from before the house was built.

Night view of the upper and lower rooms, emphasizing the staircase.

Night view of the ecological wall; inside, one can see a seventeenth-century long, narrow Tuscan table and a pair of blue-and-white seventeenth-century Albissola vases.

A view of the ecological wall. In the foreground, a vintage Charles Eames chair.

This group translates current global behavior. It is a mix that complies with Ugo di Pace's composition criteria, combining high quality heterogeneous pieces, which can be true works of art or pieces that are interesting in and of themselves. Thus, the sofa sides are lined with truck tarpaulin, complete with sewn-up rips, whereas the cushions are made from a sophisticated Rubelli fabric. By the side, there is a fully automated 1955 RAF ejection seat (an extraordinary relic), as well as a beautiful root from the Philippines, turned into a comfortable chair lined with cushions made from an antique oriental rug. The coffee table was made with seventeenth-century Florentine stone roof dogs, with iron feet and a glass top. The Coromandel screen is from the eighteenth century.

On an eighteenth-century Chinese console, a sculpture by Antonio Canova and a Chinese Tang dynasty goose.

The upper living room at night.

Upper and lower view of the living room, with
the dining room in the background.

View of the far end of the mezzanine. In the composition, in between the sofas, in lieu of a coffee table, an antique elephant saddle holds second-century BC Roman fragments.

Large wooden branch from the Philippines turned into an armchair with nineteenth-century oriental rug cushions, contrasting with the branches of the vegetation outside.

Frontal view of the upper and lower rooms.

The reading room, the lower part of which consists of bookshelves and the upper part of which consists of display windows for Roman vases from the first, second, and third centuries BC and eighteenth-century heads.

The dining room with a table made from seventeenth-century Italian capitals; eighteenth-century Chinese chairs (Ch'ien Lung); a seventeenth-century Spanish stone portal; and a wall lined with an amber-colored mirror.

A composition with a 1694 painting by Enoch Seeman; a sixteenth-century Italian marble column; an eighteenth-century baroque console; a Chinese Ming dynasty vase; a first-century BC Roman head; a seventeenth-century Venetian stool by the wood sculptor Brustolon; and an iron sculptural table with a third-century AD Roman marble fragment.

A detail view of the eighteenth-century Chinese flamingoes; 1936 Mies van der Rohe chair; and the eighteenth-century Venetian grotto chair.

Night view of the lower living room.

View through the wall of mirrors.

A detail of the ecological wall and the pool, coated with Sicis ceramic mosaic.

A view from the exterior at night, showing the ecological wall and the pool, as well as part of the interior, where one gets a glimpse of the Tang dynasty Chinese figure.

A corner of the upper and lower living rooms.

Panorama view at night from the mezzanine
of the upper level room.

Acknowledgments

Ugo di Pace Interior Design, Ugo di Pace Development, Di Pace Associated Architects, and the Modern and Classic Art Consultancy, all of which are part of the Di Pace & di Pace Group, have carried out collaborative projects over the past several years and are responsible for the works depicted in this book.

Relying on the direction and vision of Ugo di Pace, Raul di Pace, and Maria Andraus di Pace, who view the end product to be the result of the initiatives shared among these different areas of expertise, Di Pace & di Pace Associados has developed work that is the outcome of studies that seek to allow for greater creative freedom.

Freeform building designs with external columns, raised flooring, and innovative electrical and hydraulic infrastructures make virtually any type of layout possible. This approach carries the added benefit of being able to create a different facade for each floor, demonstrating a commitment to providing custom projects for each client according to his or her needs.

All apartments illustrated in this book (except the one on page 146) were developed in our freeform buildings.

www.dipace&dipace.com